AF130768

Rainer Holl

The Narrative Game

The Reading of David Foster Wallace's Infinite Jest as Play

Anchor Compact

Holl, Rainer: The Narrative Game: The Reading of David Foster Wallace's Infinite Jest as Play. Hamburg, Anchor Academic Publishing 2013
Original title of the thesis: The Reading of David Foster Wallaces "Infinite Jest" as Play

Buch-ISBN: 978-3-95489-057-6
PDF-eBook-ISBN: 978-3-95489-557-1
Druck/Herstellung: Anchor Academic Publishing, Hamburg, 2013
Additionally: Technische Universität Dortmund, Dortmund, Deutschland, Bachelorarbeit

Bibliografische Information der Deutschen Nationalbibliothek:
Die Deutsche Nationalbibliothek verzeichnet diese Publikation in der Deutschen
Nationalbibliografie; detaillierte bibliografische Daten sind im Internet über
http://dnb.d-nb.de abrufbar

Bibliographical Information of the German National Library:
The German National Library lists this publication in the German National Bibliography.
Detailed bibliographic data can be found at: http://dnb.d-nb.de

© Anchor Academic Publishing, ein Imprint der Diplomica® Verlag GmbH
http://www.diplom.de, Hamburg 2013
Printed in Germany

Table of Contents

I would like to start this paper with a quote by David Foster Wallace, the author of *Infinite Jest*, who hanged himself on September 12th 2008.

> "This is the way Barthian and Derridean post-structuralism's helped me the most as a fiction writer: once I'm done with the thing, I'm basically dead, and probably the text's dead; it becomes simply language, and language lives not just in but "through" the reader. The reader becomes God, for all textual purposes. I see your eyes glazing over, so I'll hush." (McCaffery, 1993)

I will let him maintain his silence for the rest of this paper, which will be dealing with the book that actually made his voice heard and celebrated in literary circles all around the world: *Infinite Jest*, published in 1996. What is tragic aspect about David Foster Wallace's reference to Roland Barthes' text *The Death of the Author* is that Wallace is now dead in fact. After decades of suffering from a clinical depression that he could only endure with the help of heavy medication, Wallace stopped taking these drugs because they made him even more ill than his mental illness. When his depression came back right after he was 'clean', he decided that he just could not handle life anymore. At least this seems to be a simple explanation. However, the true reasons for his *morte de se* will remain his own secret, which I will not try to reveal be finding arguments for Wallace's suicide in his literary *œuvre*. Although his texts and especially *Infinite Jest* show some parallels to the life of the author, they still remain 'language'. What this language may have meant to the author *himself* can only be experienced through the author *himself*. The reader is busy enough to deal with the text's implications on her own person anyway. In this respect, Wallace's literary death was not without a purpose. It puts the reader in a front row position, gives her all area access and makes her the mistress of the text. The text lives in and through the reader and makes it her very own; at least that is the theory. Nevertheless, the author is relieved from his responsibility for the text and is thus set free. It is a circle in which "the birth of the reader must be at the cost of the death of the author." (Barthes 1977: p.148)

The birth of the reader is also the precondition for the rebirth of the text itself. At this point I shall thus leave the author and focus my analysis on the idiosyncratic reading experience of *Infinite Jest*, which constitutes this process of textual reincarnation. But how does this actually work with a text as lengthy and complex as *Infinite Jest*? My argument is that the reading experience is mainly influenced by the internal performances of play of infinity and jest. What I will try to find out in this paper is whether the reading experience itself can also be depicted as a performance of play with the reader performing as a player. Or would it be more appropriate to speak of a game, which relies on a finite set of rules and which involves the reader as soon as she starts reading without her even realizing it? In any case, the reader has to slip into the role of a player, who is endowed with God-like textual authority, and who has to play with the different dimensions of infinity and jest, which leaves her facing some serious problems. In this paper I would like to analyze these problems and implications, explain them, and try to find possible causes for them. Furthermore, I will investigate how the various performances of play of infinity and jest influence the reader and constitute her reading experience.

The first problem the reader faces arises before reading even starts. It is the decision to actually read a book that already appears daunting due to its sheer dimensions; a book that measures 30x15x5 cm and has a shipping weight of about 1.45 kg; a book that, considering the words per page ratio of 5/3 in comparison to other more customary books, contains about 1,800 pages of condensed literature including 388 footnotes. These features almost seem anachronistic in times of EBooks and the Amazon Kindle and according to Miriam Böttger are best not mentioned if one wishes for the book to be read by many readers. (cf. Böttger 2009) The reader has to be willing to start a sort of relationship with the book that would not leave anyone unaffected who makes it through the whole text. The physical dimension of the book is the first aspect of infinity the reader is confronted with and which leaves her somehow intimidated. It is the *angst* to be out of one's depth with the book and the inability to deal with the text, which clashes with the reader's desire to be entertained.

Fortunately, the enthusiastic reader will not be dispirited so easily. Nevertheless, the dimensional and haptic aspects interfere with the reading process. One very basic implication is the need to use two bookmarks. Due to the large number of footnotes that force the reader to jump between pages, this little tool becomes almost indispensable. Another implication caused by the book's dimensions is that even the soft cover version is not apt to be read outside the house. It is not even a book that one might read in bed before going to sleep. It is a book that demands full attention and a certain amount of active reading time per day. The emphasis being on the word 'active' since *Infinite Jest* is not a recreational, passive read. Furthermore, it is quite likely that the reader will not read any other books while reading *Infinite Jest*. Depending on how fast she reads this means that the book really becomes a manifest part of her life for a couple weeks or even months (in my case almost two months). In this time the reader thinks constantly about the book and struggles with it, drawing inferences to her own life that then find their way back into the reading process. The complexity of the novel and the topics discussed in combined with the length of the book create a more intensive reader/text relationship than other books that demand lesser amounts of readingwork and energy. These implications on the reading process show that *Infinite Jest* is a book that does not just satisfy demands but also makes its own. Some of these demands might seem trivial but nevertheless they are a crucial part of the reading experience.

While on the subject of satisfying demands, it might be worth taking a closer look at the reader's expectations from the book. Whoever hopes to find a prototypical post-modern novel by one of the most celebrated writers of the whole U.S. will be let down by the very same writer who said that his texts are 'simply language' that lives through the reader alone. Thus the reader turns away from laudatory critics and everything that was written about the book in newspapers and literary journals, and just focuses on the text itself. If she turns the book over she can see from the blurb that the book is "[s]et in an addict's halfway house and a tennis academy, and featuring one of the most endearingly screwed up families in contemporary fiction." (Wallace 1996) The blurb also tells her that the book is about entertainment and the pursuit of happiness in America, and it makes her aware that she has spent her money on "one of those rare books that renew the idea of what a novel can do." (Wallace 1996) This does not fully explain to the reader what type of book this is going to be (a family drama, a junky story, a sports novel, a satire on the American entertainment society, etc.) but at least she is aware that the book seems different from other books since it "bends every rule of fiction without sacrificing its own entertainment value." (Wallace 1996) The various and more specific meanings of this 'entertainment value' definitely reach farther than what might usually be called 'fun to read'. I will elaborate on this later. For now it is sufficient to say that this information calms the reader's original fear of the book's size since it promises some sort of entertainment and thus establishes the setup for the play of infinity and jest.

In this configuration, with the reader acting as a player, the book itself becomes the essential play-ground for the reading process. By following the structuralist approach of Huizinga and Caillois, Mark Bresnan describes this play-ground as "the *langue* within which the possibilities for play are limitless – as long as the boundaries themselves are not violated." (Bresnan 2008: p. 52) Conversely, in the post-structuralist view of Jacques Derrida on the contrary, it is not the totalization of a limited set of boundaries but rather the non-totalization that determine the concept of play. (cf. Derrida 1966: p.161) So the autonomy of the player or in our case the reader "is produced by the disruption of a system rather than by adherence to its rules and boundaries." (Bresnan 2008: p.53) An interesting question related to *Infinite Jest* is to what extent the reader is able to establish and defend her own rules and boundaries that are challenged by her discourse with the book. This opens up a new dimension of play which has an immediate impact on the autonomy of the reader. The haptic features of the book for example are a performance of play in which infinity challenges jest in terms of complexity versus the value of enter-tainment for the reader. The reader herself is again engaged in this performance as she is forced to adapt her reading habits to the structure of the book.

Besides the noteable physical dimension, the next thing that strikes the reader after she has started reading is the structural idiosyncrasy of the book. It starts with the fact that there is hardly any way to successfully summarize this book. Yes, there is the Enfield Tennis Academy, the Ennet Halfway-House, the future of American 'experialism', of Subsidized Time and of anti-American terror cells, and there is of course the movie *Infinite Jest*, which is lethally addictive, perfect entertainment. And yet there is always one more piece of the puzzle that is missing, one more undetected or rather unexpected level, one more mind-twisting challenge for the reader that she can or cannot accept. In order to make this complicated plot actually tellable, the story has to be narrated by various different narrators, some of which are more trustworthy than others.

The first chapter is narrated from the 1st person view of Hal Incanden-za, a young tennis prodigy and one of the book's protagonists, describing a weird application interview with a university headmaster. Hal confronts the reader with a lot of information that makes her aware of his slightly shifted point of view that somehow constantly prevents her from getting a full picture of the situation. All of his observations are concerned with superficial things like "[t]he yellow Dean's eyebrows [that] go circumflex," or "[t]he two halves of his moustache that never quite match." (p.4) On page 6 Hal evaluates everything that is said to him in terms of linguistic correctness rather than in terms of its actual contextual meaning, namely his application for the tennis academy. Despite some uncertainty that the reader experiences, she might still condone this situation since it is only the first chapter and there are more than a thousand pages to go. But this feeling of textual wobbliness will remain a central part of the reading experience throughout the text. Either the narrators conceal important information from the reader or they hide it in a heap of seemingly unim-portant information which makes it even harder to figure out what is going on and advance to the centre. One could even argue that it is in fact impossible to ever reach the centre since this would mean the end of play and the existential end of the text itself. That is because the centre "closes off the play which it opens up and makes possible. As centre, it is the point at which the substitution of contents, elements, or terms is no longer possible." (Derrida 1966:p.150) The only centre that the text offers is the lethally addictive entertainment; the movie *Infinite Jest*.

This movie, which was made by Hal's father, James O. Incandenza, is so entertaining that anyone it captivates can do nothing but watch it over and over again till they finally die on their sofa. In this singularity the play of infinity and jest finds its perfection and its end. But for the reader this is only a concept just like the concept of death itself. It can only be described from an outsider's point of view since no one who has ever seen that movie is actually able to talk about it. There is not even anything like near-infinite-jest experiences. This strange situation coincides with Derrida's definition of the term "centre [which] is, paradoxically, *within* the structure and *outside* it." (Derrida 1966:p.150) The play of infinity is performed here by recursion, a never-ending, self-referential process that is marked by stasis since once this centre is reached, nothing essential will happen anymore. The ultimate realization of the play between infinity and jest would be equal to the end of the reader and of play itself. Therefore, the reader only gets hints as to what the centre, namely the movie, might look like. This constant state of uncertainty is why the reader never loses the notion of textual anxiety, which "is invariably the result of a certain mode of being implicated in the game, of being caught by the game" (Derrida 1966: p.151)

The movie 'Infinite Jest' is not the only realization of the concept of recursion in the book. The whole book is actually structured in this man-ner. "*Infinite Jest* creates cycles within cycles within cycles. Imagine a huge novel that has been run through [...] recursive feedback loops [...] and then strung out along the page." (Hayles 1999:p.684) This becomes apparent through changes of the narrative situation, irregular time shifts, a large number of characters, and an extreme linguistic diversity. This confronts the reader with a massive amount of information that she has to process while she is working herself through this system of cycles. For the German critic Wieland Freund, Wallace's book is the first big novel of the *Wissensgesellschaft*. "In *Infinite Jest* all regulators are to boost, all data tracks are active; you get a bonus-track to the bonus-track and a making-of of the making-of plus extra material and endnotes." (Freund 2009) The first reference to the almost 100 pages of "NOTES AND ERRATA", which leads the reader to page 983, appears on page 23. It tells the reader that "Methamphetamine hydrochloride [is also known as] crystal meth." (p.983) Some of the information that the reader extracts from the endnotes are not really necessary in order to understand the text. Sometimes they even have the opposite effect and supply the reader with information that is so complex that she becomes over-saturated. Endnote 12 for example describes Demerol and Talwin as "Meperedine hydrochloride and penta-zocine hydrochloride, Schedule C-II and C-IV[a] narcotic analgesics, respectively, both from the good old folks over at Sanofi Winthrop Pharm-Labs, Inc." (p.984) The little [a] behind C-IV actually refers to a footnote belonging to that endnote, which gives further information about the Continental Controlled Substance Act. Anyone without a degree in organic chemistry or a serious drug habit would have no idea what this piece of information is about. Still, the reader is not totally deterred by the endnote since the expression 'good old folks' builds up a colloquial antipode to those scientific expressions and thus defangs the whole paragraph. This is a linguistic twist that transfers meanings rather implicitly so that the reader gets a general idea what is going on but is basically left in the vague, tangled mass of over-information.

This becomes apparent no later than when the reader reaches end-note 24, which is a complete filmography of James O. Incandenza, Hal's late father. This detailed summary of J.O.I.'s *œuvre* extends over 8 densely filled pages. Now the reader realizes that the endnotes have to be seen as more than just a supplement to the text. Their entity almost represents an entirely different book, not just including comments and explanations of special terms but sometimes whole chapters that continue the plot of the novel. Endnote number 110 is a whole 12 page long chapter about Hal talking to his brother Orin on the telephone. Orin no longer lives with his family and has rejected all his mother's attempts to get in touch with him. The text shows this with "A MOVING EXAMPLE OF THE SORTS OF PHYSICAL POST MAIL MRS. INCANDENZA HAS SENT TO HER ELDEST CHILD ORIN [...]" (p.1006), which is answered by "AN EXAMPLE OF THE INVARIANT RESPONSE THESE PIECES OF MAIL ELICIT". (p.1007).

This response is presented in the text in the form of a typewritten telegram to underline Orin's strong rejection and unresponsiveness. After this, the conversation between Orin and Hal continues. The whole endnote is structured like an evidence record collecting arguments and information from different sources in order to prove something to the reader. In other cases the endnotes have the opposite function and disprove what was mentioned in the text.

Endnote 49 for example refers to the text passage where information about the "Ennet House Drug and Alcohol Recovery House" (p.137) is given and calls this expression wrong for its "Redundancy *sic*". (p. 995) On page 787, there even appears an endnote ([324]) which has no textual reference at all, but just stands between two paragraphs making it look almost like a headline. Thus, the endnotes gain autonomy from the actual text.

The 388 endnotes form another recursive and self-referential cycle within the text, in which the reader constantly moves around and sometimes even gets lost. The most significant feature of this cycle is its functional duality. On the one hand it represents a constitutional part of the text itself; on the other hand it creates some sort of meta-fiction that challenges the text and thus performs a play of meaning. This play is constituted by the seemingly infinite amount of different and sometimes even contradicting information that the reader has to deal with. This flood of information is the reader's personal 'Too Much' which connects her to almost any other character in the book, each of which is suffering from their personal 'Too Much' as well. J.O.I.'s "Too Much [for example] was

neat bourbon, and he lived life to the fullest, and then gone in for detoxification again and again." (p.235) The reader's recursive cycling through
the text and the inability to surface from the mass of information presented
to her is analogous to the constant, ineffective struggle of the book's
characters to overcome their personal Too Much, mostly represented by
their addiction to a certain substance.

The reader of *Infinite Jest* can be classified into the same category as
those characters since her own reading experience features symptoms of
an increasing addiction as well.

> "Infinite Jest not only describes the contemporary culture of addiction
> in the USA but produces, through its exhilaratingly tortuous narrative,
> a reading experience that resembles addiction. The book, in other
> words, is like a drug." (Aubry 2008: p.208)

The structural complexity that intimidated the reader in the beginning is
actually keeps her hanging on now. The way this literary drug works is in
fact the same as with chemical substances. The consumer enters a short
but very pleasant state of mental well-being and shows serious withdrawal
symptoms when this stimulus is taken away. The novel does this by
interrupting the line of action whenever the reader might have started to
feel comfortable or a scene has almost reached its dramatic climax. On
page 601 for example the reader gets a very detailed inside view into a
typical night shift of Don Gately, Ennet-House in-house staffer, recovering
drug addict, and the novel's second main character. Every night, Gately
has the wearisome job of making every house resident move their car to
another parking lot since the city of Boston has made "this hellish munici-
pal deal where only one side of any street is illegal for parking, and the
legal side switches abruptly at 0000h." (p.602) This episode is narrated in
the present tense and stretches over 8 pages, which gives the reader
quite a good idea of the tediousness of this task. The reading itself becomes wearisome and the reader craves for narrative action. Then
suddenly, on page 608, the scene actually turns into the most exciting
episode of the whole book when a group of young Canadians try to kill
one of Gately's residents who had killed their dog previously. The narra-

tive action works here like a drug that awakens the reader as well as Gately, who "gets very cool and clear and his headache recedes and his breathing slows. It is not so much that things slow as break into frames." (p.608) The over-detailed and lengthy passage thus turns into a thrilling fighting scene at the end of which Gately is wounded by a shotgun. On page 618 the scene is suddenly interrupted by technical information about entertainment technology and without clearing up what happens to Gately, leaving an excited reader who will have to wait another 130 pages till this line of action continues. It is the play of stasis and entertainment in the broadest sense, the fact that "everything always speeds up and slows down both" (p.612), which makes the reading so addictive.

With regards to its content and structural complexity, *Infinite Jest* builds up "parallels between consuming drugs and consuming infor-mation." (Aubrey 2008: p.208) In terms of chemical substances, there is always the risk of losing control over the habit and dying of an over-dosage of the particular substance. Similarly, the text with its high density of information being the substance of addiction, the reader is also in the constant danger of injecting more information than she can actually handle. No later than at this point should it become clear that the perfor-mance of play in *Infinite Jest* is also a play of power relations between the text and the reader. At the point where the reader risks losing control, the performance of play actually turns into a game in which the text challeng-es its consumer in terms of authority.

The concept of game brings me back to Hal Incandenza who is a young, talented tennis prodigy at the Enfield Tennis Academy, an elite tennis high school for future professional players. According to Sven Birkerts, the E.T.A. is a world where "nothing much happens;" "a game world, a closed system, [from which] the idea of play has been pumped out of." (Birkerts 1996) This does not sound very entertaining at first and casts doubt the dramaturgic value of this plot line. But the infinite jest can even be found in the dreary routine of a junior tennis academy. At this point it is worth consulting an etymological dictionary to find out a little more about this old fashioned word 'jest' and which strange meanings it actually adopts in the book. Origins Short Etymological Dictionary describes 'jest' as a derivative from the Latin stem 'gerere', which amongst others means 'to perform'. 'Jest' is also related to the French word 'geste', which is a 'tale of exploits'. This information gives some hints to the reader as to the type of narrative that she has to deal with; the narrative of everyday life. This narrative can be described as relatively "eventless, whereas the lives of the characters we follow in narrative fiction are eventful and highly charged." (Berger 1997: p.162) The 'jest' or rather the 'performance' aspect in this type of narrative takes the form of *repeat performances*.

In our everyday life just as in E.T.A., these performances "spare us from having to exert energy and make decisions about relatively trivial matters every day." (Berger 1997: p. 162) The recurring character of these performances thus depicts another form of play between infinity and jest. It is the play of everyday routine and life's daily challenges that accompanies us until the end of our life. At E.T.A. those routines or rather *repeat performances* are highly structured and consist of "A.M. drills, shower, eat, class, class, eat, […], lab/class, conditioning run, P.M. drills, play challenge match, play challenge match, upper body circuits in weight room, sauna, shower, slump to locker-room floor w/ other players." (p.95) This cycle of planned routine relates to further features of everyday life narratives. The first one is that there is no beginning, middle, or end. Everything is preceded and succeeded, everything is the middle. The implication for the reader is that it becomes difficult for her to focus on one particular issue in this construct. This especially includes potential conflicts that remain muted and only appear randomly, or the character's aims concerning the resolution of these conflicts that remain rather vague. (cf. Berger 1997: p.162)

At E.T.A. everyone gets told which aims they should focus on. This is basically to make it to 'The Show' one day and become a successful tennis pro. The way to reach this goal is virtually entirely predefined and does not leave much room for variation or deviation. This becomes clear to the reader in one episode of the book, in which the narrator describes a short movie called "TENNIS AND THE FERAL PRODIGY." (p.172) This movie is structured into little 'Here is how to...' scenes that describe meticulously how everything at E.T.A. has to be done in order to succeed. One of the most important things here is not to question any of those guidelines.

> "Here is how to avoid thinking about any of this by practicing and playing until everything runs on autopilot and talent's unconscious exercise becomes a way to escape yourself, a long walking dream of pure play." (p.173)

This quote describes one of the secret aims of E.T.A. that is manifested in the hidden curriculum. It is the aim to turn self-determined, young individuals into some sort of maximum-efficiency tennis machines that just act rather than react. The play of infinity and jest, namely the continuous repetition of pre-determined performances, is used here to transform unique characters into stock characters whose literary performance is to act out what was indoctrinated into them. This is rather contradictory in terms of play since this transformation seems to limit the performance of play within the characters. But according to E.T.A. philosophy, this is the only way to become a successful tennis player. In order to solve this paradox, it is necessary to take a closer look at the different performances of play in professional competitive tennis in *Infinite Jest*.

The seemingly limitless character of play governed by a finite set of rules is a setup that does not work in *Infinite Jest's* world of sports. "[T]he operative structures governing play go well beyond the 'rules of the game', encompassing [...] many other forces." (Bresnan 2008: p.53) The players at E.T.A. are less taught how to *play* the game but rather how to *live* the game. According to Bresnan, "sports and play are depicted throughout the novel as entirely discrete endeavors." (Bresnan 2008: p.56) This becomes clear if one takes a look at Caillois' definition of playful activities that should be separate from everyday life, voluntary, uncertain in outcome and unproductive (cf. Bresnan 2008:p.56) At E.T.A. play is inextricably connected with everyday life. This also makes it also far from being voluntary. If the players stop playing, they will get dismissed from the academy. Either the player is fully involved or not at all. There are no half-measures. This resembles the idiosyncratic reading experience of the reader.

Reading an incredibly complex book like *Infinite Jest* also leaves the reader with two choices. Either she totally immerses herself in the complex narrative(s) or she refuses to. This can be compared to Lenz's theory regarding police sirens. When Lenz, a relapsing drug addict, is on his way home from an Alcoholic Anonymous meeting he muses that police sirens always either sound "terribly achingly far away [...] or they're on your ass. No middle distance with sirens." (p.543) So as soon as the book is "on the reader's ass" it is not separate from her everyday life anymore. The combination of the narrative of everyday life with the relatively long reading time eliminates the middle distance between the book and the reader. Just like the players at E.T.A. she is not just playing the game, but living it. Considering the addictive qualities of the text, the reading even loses its voluntariness. Although the outcome is still unclear, she feels that she has to continue and make it through the text. Due to the loss of its liberating character, reading of the novel, just like play in general actually becomes work.

In presenting play at E.T.A. as work, *Infinite Jest* follows a "tradition within postmodern literature that questions the connection between sports and liberating play." (Bresnan 2008: p.54) Because of the infiniteness of this routine, play has no beginning and no end; it is simply always present and therefore, not at all. Furthermore, this form of play is characterized by its division into two dueling ranges, which pick up the competitive dimension of sports and transform life at E.T.A. into a constant gaming performance. In this game the original beauty of tennis has to compete with the operational business structures of the professional sports. Tennis itself turns into a branch of the entertainment industry, a serious business in which the sporting competition is only subordinate. In order to succeed in this business, the children at E.T.A. learn to fight their ego early on, and set everything personal aside. Everything apart from tennis and the irrepressible will to make it to "The Show [where] they'll be entertainers." (p.661).

This opens up another battlefield of this game, which is the struggle of growing up with all its usual implications versus the difficulty of meeting the high expectations of playing competitive tennis on a national scale. It is a game in which the players have to give up something in order to win something else, even if this means losing their teenage years. Nevertheless, the game with intrinsic duality is what makes everyday life at E.T.A. actually tellable and interesting to the reader. Due to its narrative qualities, the tennis plot involving Hal Incandenza could be classified as a *Bildungsroman*, but in relation to the etymological meanings of 'jest' I would rather describe it as a 'tale of exploits'.

The most apparent exploitation at E.T.A. takes the form of extreme physical and mental exhaustion and the total utilization of the students for their future in the professional tennis business. But the more fundamental and yet profound exploitation of the children is shown in the loss of their personality as a sacrifice for their career. The kids become mere objects of entertainment value for The Show. They become objects that the audiences "can project themselves onto, forgetting their own limitations in the face of the nearly limitless potential someone as young [as the kids] represent." (p.524) This doctrine that was created by James O. Incandenza, Hal's father and also founder of the Enfield Tennis Academy, is based on the advice that J.O.I.'s father, also a very talented but failed tennis player, gave to his son. He taught the young James to treat every object as an important and sensible being. His example for the ill-usage of objects was Marlon Brando, "the archetypal tough-guy rebel and slob type [...] trying to dominate objects, showing no artful respect or care." (p.157) This philosophy contradicted James' father's view, who thought that every object should be treated with great respect in order to make it respond. He even goes so far as to describe people as mere objects in the shape of human bodies.

> "Commit this to memory. Head is body. Jim, brace yourself against my shoulders here for this hard news at ten: you're a machine a body an object, Jim, no less than this." (p.159)

14

From early on, the child learns that it is rather a mechanic being that has to function in a certain way instead of a sensible and thinking being that has feelings and emotions. For J.O.I.'s father, everything belonging to the realm of mental activities is "just neural spasms, those thoughts in [the] mind are just the sound of [the] head revving, and head is still just body." (p.159) In this context it is no wonder that the most talented and top-ranked player at E.T.A., John Wayne is described as a "grim machine." (p.438) His mechanic features are that he plays highly efficient tennis, is as good as indefatigable, and shows almost no emotional involvement whatsoever. His emotional emptiness does not just represent the final educational aim of E.T.A.; it also resembles the ultimate body: "a tennis ball [...]. Perfectly round. Even distribution of mass. But empty inside, utterly, a vacuum. Susceptible to whim, spin, to force – used well or poorly. It will reflect your own character. " (p.160) The perfect E.T.A. student, just like a tennis ball, represents pure potential that can be released with just the right treatment of force or spin. Nevertheless, the emptiness inside the student's mind remains the prerequisite for this process. Once they have reached this status they will be "barely aware of what [they're] doing. [Their] body is doing it for [them] and the court and the Game is doing it for [their] body." (p.166) Thus, the game itself actually takes control over the body. The body becomes detached from the mind and becomes the executive instance of a legislative game that takes the place of the mind.

Once again, there is a parallel between the characters in the book, namely the E.T.A. students as players of this game, and the reader of *Infinite Jest*. Since the reading experience of the novel resembles a game situation and assuming that the reader herself is a living object that can also be depicted as some sort of body, the theory of J.O.I.'s father applies here as well. The book being the essential play-ground, or in this case rather the court of the game, has a legislative influence on the reading habits and the reading experiences of the reader, who herself turns into the executive unit, performing this given game. So the reader is chal-lenged by the book through her performance of reading. Interestingly enough, the book is not the reader's opponent in this game. In fact there is no opponent at all. According to Gerhard Schtitt, the German chief coach at E.T.A., the opponent in tennis is just the *excuse* or the *occasion* to play. The actual opponent of each player is their own ego. In Schtitt's opinion "[y]ou compete with your own limits to transcend the self in imagination and execution. Disappear inside the game: break through limits: transcend: improve: win." (p.84) For the consumer of the book this means that she has to transcend herself by her totally disappearing into the game, which is the reading experience. This sort of game is "not a fractal matter of reducing chaos to pattern." (p.82)

The chaos or rather the complexity of the book is nothing that should or could anyhow be governed by the reader. It is an

> "infinity of infinites of choice and execution, mathematically un-
> controlled but humanly contained, bounded by the talent and imagi-
> nation of self and opponent, bent in on itself by the containing
> boundaries of skill and imagination that brought one player finally
> down, that kept both from winning, that made it, finally, a game,
> these boundaries of self." (p.82)

In this compact paragraph, Schtitt describes the self-competitive character of playing tennis, which is uncannily similar to the reading of the novel depicted as a game. The complexity of the game in this case just mirrors the same structural complexity that is contained in every human being. So the reader, who struggles with the structural complexity of the book, is actually just struggling with her own dimension of inverted infiniteness. The book is just the excuse or the occasion for this game in which the reader actually meets herself as her own opponent. The irony here is that the reader can actually never win this game since this would mean ultimate self-transcendence und total disappearance into the book, which would mean the loss of her self-determinedness and thus her own end.

That is probably why Mario, Hal's deformed brother and a good friend of Schtitt, asks the coach "[w]hat's the difference between tennis and suicide, life and death, the game and its own end." (p.84) The answer might be that there probably is none; that the reading of the novel goes down with the literary death of the reader; that thus, the game destroys itself since it only exists through the reader. Lucky is the reader who is aware of her own limitations in this game and is thus able to save herself from total immersion into her personal Too Much, which would mean her ultimate disappearance. This ironic antagonism of surrendering or giving in to a certain extent in order to win, even if winning just means surviving, is also depicted in E.T.A.'s founding motto which reads "The man who knows his limitations has none." (p.81)

All this theory might sound a little bit puzzling and over-exaggerated, but it may not be forgotten that it was excogitated by J.O.I., a genius and a madman who killed himself by putting his head into a microwave oven. Nevertheless, his philosophic conception to the game represents the fundamental doctrine of everyday living for the students in the world of the Enfield Tennis Academy including Hal Incandenza. E.T.A.'s educational approach to facilitate the process of self-transcendence is characterized by suffering and pain. What sounds cruel at first is actually meant to protect the children from the mechanism of the game, which is "the machine they are all dying to throw themselves into." (p.661) In this machine the children become statues that are looked upon by the audiences. The game itself becomes incidental for these onlookers, who are only interested in entertainment and personality. The E.T.A. students however get "inculcated their sense that it's never about being seen," so that "they can forget everything but the game" and will "never be slaves to the statue." (p.661) Strangely enough, the game itself is what protects the kids from its own implicated dangers. But in order to make this work, the students have to lose themselves completely in the game, which is "something bigger than them. To have it stay the way it was when they started, the game as something bigger." (p.660)

The actual dimension of this game becomes clear in a very unpleasant and recurring dream from which Hal woke up each night for a couple of weeks. In this dream Hal is standing on a really huge tennis court where he is involved in a competitive match and surrounded by spectators and officials. This dream is an impressive description of the game's complexity that is worth quoting at length.

> "The court is about the size of a football field, though, maybe, it seems. It's hard to tell. But mainly the court's complex. The lines that bound and define play are on this court as complex and convolved as a sculpture of string. There are lines going every which way, and they run oblique or meet and form relationships and boxes and rivers and tributaries and systems inside systems: lines, corners, alleys, and angles deliquesce into a blur at the horizon of the distant net." (p.67)

Hal's dream stages another performance of play between infinity and jest. The infinity aspect is represented through the complexity of the game that makes it actually impossible to play at all. The game can thus never start and nullifies itself through its own complex rules and regulations. But, probably because of the audience's demand for entertainment, Hal and his opponent start to play anyway. At least they pretend to. "But it's all hypothetical, somehow. Even the 'we' is theory: I never get quite to see the distant opponent, for all the apparatus of the game." (p.68) Hal is not just overwhelmed by the surrounding apparatus of the game; he does not even have an essential excuse to play at all because he is not able to identify his opponent. Since the real opponent in competitive tennis is the player himself, we could assume that Hal was suffering from some sort of identity crisis when he had these dreams.

But Hal is not the only one who has to deal with this problem. *Infinite Jest*, this gargantuan novel, is also marked by its infinite complexity and plot lines that go in every possible direction. This literary play-ground less resembles a tennis court or a football field but rather a golf course that features various different holes; each being somehow unique and yet indirectly connected to one another. The connections between these different sites are so confusing that the reader is tempted to get lost in that system. Her reading would then become the hypothetical and theoretical play of Hal's dream in which she would not even know whom she is playing with or that she is playing at all.

Hal's life however is not the game of reading a book but the hard and exhausting life of a young E.T.A. student. Though it was difficult for him in his dream to figure out where he was standing in the overwhelming complexity of the game, he knows exactly where he stands in the internal tennis hierarchy of the academy. This hierarchical "system's got inequality as an axiom" so that everybody "know[s] just where [they] stand at all times." (p.112) The fear of mediocrity, of failing in this system and even getting statistical evidence for this transforms life at E.T.A. into "a kind of reverse-Buddhism, a state of Total Worry." (p.451) The focus on individual performance demands combined with the fact that these young kids live together relatively close, creates another dimension of play, which the students call "a community-spiel." (p.112)

In this community the constant suffering and fear is what actually unites the group and sharpens its focus. Again, it is Hal who finds the right description for this condition.

> "The suffering *unites* us. They want to let us sit around and bitch. Together. After a bad P.M. set we all, however briefly, get to feel we have a common enemy. This is their gift to us. Their medicine. Nothing brings you together like a common enemy." (p.113)

Even if this common enemy, which is of course the board of E.T.A. officials and the coach staff, is just a substitute, it nevertheless replaces the blurry blank spot where the opponent is supposed to be in the complex apparatus of the game. The passages in the book in which Hal talks about this complexity, are where the reader gets the opportunity 'to bitch' with him about this issue. The complexity of the game or rather the reading experience becomes the common enemy of Hal and the reader and fills the blank that would make the reading game hypothetical and senseless. The complexity thus becomes an integral part of the game and the danger of getting lost becomes smaller. The community play of the Enfield Tennis Academy even involves the reader and makes her an accomplice, which in return helps her to improve in her role as a player of *Infinite Jest*.

Despite the fact that Hal shares his life at E.T.A. with dozens of other players, he remains as lonesome as the reader herself. The community at E.T.A. is not based on empathy and mutual assistance, but on a constant state of competition and contest. For Hal personally everything in his life is a contest. After he found his dad with his head exploded in a microwave, Hal did not show any signs of psychic pain or mental disorder. This made the Moms (Hal's, Orin's and Mario's nickname for their mother) quite suspicious and so she decided to send her son to see a grief-therapist. In fact, because Hal did not feel any grief, he was not able to deliver the therapist any goods. This made Hal worried since he "never failed to deliver the goods before." (p.253) Hal was less concerned with the dramatic death of his father than with the fear of "somehow going to flunk grief-therapy." (p.254) So in the end, J.O.I.'s death still made Hal suffer but only in terms of the fear of not meeting other people's expectations. Hal actually overcomes this particular situation by reading several books about grief therapy in order to specify these specific expectations. After that he stages a dramatic spectacle to the therapist where he fakes a grief-therapist textbook moment of epiphany in which he admits that his first unconscious thought immediately before finding his father was "[t]*hat something smelled delicious!*" (p.256)

But Hal's final relief from the constant state of Total Worry, from the never-ending competition and the pressure to succeed, did not come from a textbook for young E.T.A. students but from the redeeming smoke of a loaded hash pipe. The whole complex of the Enfield Tennis Academy is pervaded by a complicated underground tunnel system. This is the place where Hal regularly hides in order to secretly smoke marijuana. "Hal likes to get high in secret, but a bigger secret is that he's as attached to the secrecy as he is to getting high." (p.49) The fact that he is doing something which is not approved of by the academy or the Moms, who is also the female's headmistress at E.T.A., makes his drug habit a form of liberating play. He returns to the tunnel system of his own will and thus purposely breaks the rules of the game that apply on the surface. Although this form of play gives him short relief from the pressure at the Academy it is not liberating play per se. On the one hand he actually needs it in order to survive at E.T.A., but on the other hand he just slips into another dominating game; the game of addiction. This addiction is not rooted in the psychic or physical dependence on a chemical substance but in the secrecy of the game itself. The official rules of the game at E.T.A. thus resemble Huizinga and Caillois' structuralist approach of limitless play within a finite set of boundaries whereas Hal's secret play is more similar to Derrida's post-structural disruption of this system.

This performance of play is the only thing that can really liberate Hal from his own ego. He does not just lose Himself, which is the nickname of his father J.O.I., but also himself in terms of his self-determinedness. He ends up getting lost in a game that actually consists of a play of two different games; the regulated life at E.T.A. and Hal's drug habit. The loss of Hal's autonomy becomes clear in a shift of the narrative situation. The episodes in the book where Hal struggles with his life at E.T.A. and is not under the influence of any kind of substances are narrated by Hal himself as a 1st person narrator. "I am in here." (p.3) This quote mirrors Hal's ability to speak for himself as well as his state of being captured in his own mind. All of Hal's other appearances are narrated by a 3rd person narrator, which connects Hal's mental 'freedom' to his inability to speak for himself. "Here is Hal Incandenza, age seventeen, with his little brass one-hitter, getting covertly high in the Enfield Tennis Academy's underground Pump Room." (p.49) The loss of Hal's narrative authority and his self-determinedness leaves room for the game itself to take control over Hal's body. Interestingly enough, this is nothing but the consistent implementation of the E.T.A. tennis philosophy in which the kids are supposed to lose themselves in something bigger than them and let the game take the place of the mind.

This is probably why Hal's drug habit goes hand in hand with an enormous leap forward in his tennis skills, which places him on the second rank in the E.T.A. hierarchy right behind the 'grim machine' John Wayne. Hal finds a way to forget all his sorrows and fears by leaving behind his own self. In this mental state he becomes the perfect E.T.A. tennis player that can transcend the game, get lost in it and thus find shelter from the cruel world outside. The tennis court, a small parallel universe of 23.8 meters by 8.2 meters, becomes his refuge to which his drug habit is the admission fee. In this parallel world, there is nothing but the game. The whole existence of this space is founded on the rules of the game, which in return depends on the existence of this space. Coach Schtitt describes it like this

> "You have a chance to *occur*, playing. No? To make for you this second world that is always the same: there is opponent with his tool, and always only two of you, you and this other, inside the lines, with always a purpose to keep this world alive, yes?" (p.459)

Hal's disruptive drug-play that flaws the official rules of E.T.A. actually enables him to get lost in a world that is so simplified and regulated that he has to do nothing but play according to these simple regulations. He is still not free in that system, but at least it is so simple and uncomplicated enough that he is able to *occur* and start playing. Hal's loss in that system takes away his fear that the game becomes hypothetical. Theory turns into practice and transforms Hal into the second best player of the Enfield Tennis Academy.

Is Hal's strategy now good advice for the reader? For some readers the reading experience might become even more thrilling after the consumption of certain mind-expanding substances. For others the book is already addictive and thrilling enough to realize that it actually might be bigger than the reader herself. By simply considering the fact that the reader is confronted with a massive amount of characters throughout the book that counts into the hundreds, it becomes obvious that this reading game deserves some special strategies. One of those strategies could in fact be to do the same as Hal and leave the self behind. Thus, the reader is actually able to slip into the numerous characters whose destiny is presented to her through the voice of several narrators. Instead of being overwhelmed by the book's complexity the reader can just focus on the most basic regulations of this game; namely that there is a book and there is a reader, only the two of them inside a play-ground which is reason enough to keep this play-ground alive. This play-ground is the book itself and reading it becomes its own purpose. Here we can apply another etymological meaning of 'jest' which is also derived from the stem 'gerere' and which means 'being carried'. The game is established through the book and the reader which carry each other in an infinite circle. The book is being carried by the reader who is being carried the book, etc. This fragile building is another play between infinity and jest that, on the one hand, carries the reader through the book and on the other hand carries Hal to the court day after day, enabling him to occur in the game.

This changes when every E.T.A. player is forced to give a urine sample, which coerces Hal to stop taking drugs. Before that point Hal was not just a very talented tennis player but also an academic prodigy. At a very young age he had started to learn dictionaries by heart, meaning he could probably also have given detailed etymological definitions of the word 'jest'. Furthermore, he did not just read but even 'digested' whole libraries of books, which enabled him to write essays like "The Implications of Post-Fourier Transformations for a Holographically Mimetic Cinema." (p.7)

Hal is playing a game that can be described as an infinite jest in so far as he is constantly consuming and digesting knowledge just as if he were a wandering vacuum, sucking up everything around him just to fill up an inner gap.

Hal's hunger for knowledge was only topped by his appetite for food that was exceptionally huge after he smoked dope. Immediately after Hal stops to secretly smoking marijuana he does not just suffer the loss of his tennis skills but also the disappearance of his appetite. This becomes clear when he almost loses a match against Ortho Stice, a younger but also talented player that everyone calls 'The Darkness'. Considering the etymology of the name Incandenza, which is 'glowing white light', their match can in fact be seen as light vs. darkness. Hal wins the match but he realizes that something went terribly wrong. This process is symbolized when Hal is sitting at the dinner table after the match, curiously not very hungry, and Stice steals a tomato from Hal's plate "trying to respect this object with all his might." (p.637) Stice does not know what happened during the match but he realizes that "Hal had played with the wide-eyed but unfocused look of a tennis player right on the verge of falling apart out there." (p.637) When Hal finally meets his coach to recapitulate the match he gets the sobering feedback that he "just never quite occurred out there." (p.686)

This is a shock for Hal after which he starts having bad dreams again. His brother Mario wakes him up one night from a dream during which he was constantly saying "Thank you Sir may I have another," which stands for his high functionality and shows his infinite digestion of knowledge. But in the same dream Hal was losing his teeth, which made him incapable of consuming further and thus hindered him to deliver himself the goods that he was relying on. As a consequence, Hal is excluded from the game that makes it possible for him to exist because it carried him. In his real life, Hal is also carried by the game, with the tennis court symbolizing his sheltering refuge. His drug habit was the admission fee, which made it possible for him to enter this space in which he now cannot occur any-more. The abstinence creates a hole in Hal's life that threatens to suck him up. "I feel a hole. It's going to be a huge hole, in a month. A way more than Halsized hole." (p.785) Instead of being safe in the world of the game, Hal is caught "inside his own hull," (p.694) which hinders him from occurring outside and which surrenders him to a world that he is not able to cope with.

In this world Hal gets panic attacks at the mere thought of the "incred-ible volume of food [he] was going to have to consume over the rest of [his] life. Meal after meal plus snacks. Day after day." (p.897) This fear attacks the play of infinity and jest that determined his whole former life. In this new situation "[e]verything came at too many frames per second. Everything had too many aspects." (p.896) The complexity of the world that Hal successfully escaped from before this point strikes back and tears him down.

> "There seemed to be too many implications even to thinking about sitting up and standing up and exiting V.R.5 and taking a certain variable-according-to-stride-length number of steps to the stairwell door, on and on, that just the thought of getting up made me glad I was lying on the floor." (p.900)

Hal is suffering from the same sickness as the hero in John Bath's *The End of the Road,* who also decided that there was no point to doing anything anymore.

> "There was no reason to do anything. [...] It is the malady *cosmopsis*, the cosmic view, that afflicted me. When one has it, one is frozen like the bullfrog when the hunter's light strikes him full in the eyes, only with *cosmopsis* there is no hunter, and no quick hand to terminate the moment – there's only the light." (Barth 1958: p.323)

Since this "paralysis is not always total," (Noland 1966: p.245) we can describe Hal as a victim of complete *cosmopsis*. He is suffering from the cosmic view that confronts him with the manifold implications of each of his actions. He cannot even answer his fellow students when they ask him what is wrong because there are "too many potential responses, both witty ones and earnest ones" so that Hal finally decides to answer "almost at random." (p.908)

Hal's lethargy and his inability to move resemble a new kind of fictional hero. After the hero of action who plainly "is what he does", and the rather post-modern hero of re-action, Hal becomes the future "hero of non-action, the catatonic hero, the one beyond calm, divorced from all stimulus." (p.142) This hero is not even able to deal with the simplest aspects of everyday life, namely our daily decisions that we process through *repeat performances*. Since he was suffering from cosmopsis, Hal could not make decisions any more or carry out even the simplest *repeat performances*. He reaches and becomes trapped in the Derridean centre where no substitution is possible and every play has to end.

> "It occurred to me then with some force that I didn't want to play this afternoon [...] Not even neutral, I realized. I would on the whole have preferred not to play. [...] Never have to, never get to. I could be the faultless victim of a freak accident and be knocked from the game while still on the ascendant. Becoming the object of compassionate sorrow rather than disappointed sorrow." (p.954 f)

Hal's "non-identity of cosmopsis," (Noland 1966: p.246), and his inability to play, perfectly reflect Derrida's thesis that "anxiety is invariably the result of being implicated in the game." (Derrida 1966: p.151) Hal refuses to be a part of this game anymore because he fears failure and disappointing people who believed in him. He deliberately abandons the game by becoming a non-action hero who hopes to arouse other people's compassion.

The novel leaves Hal's plot-line right after he has reached the Derridean centre. At this point Hal is finally caught inside his own hull from which he cannot escape. But this is only partly true since the centre "can be either inside or outside [and] can also indifferently be called the origin or end, *archē* or *telos*." (Derrida 1966: p.151) Interestingly enough, it turns out that the first episode of the novel is actually the last part of Hal's plot-line since it is set after Hal's leaving the game and entering the centre. Hal's alleged end drives the reader back to the start and so becomes the origin of the whole novel. This circular narrative construction is a performance of play that has an immediate impact on the reader. The unusual arrangement of the book resembles the structure of a Möbius strip on which the reader wanders along while she is reading. On this curious 2–dimensional geometric form she can start walking or rather reading along the plane surface, which will first lead her to the other side of the strip and, if she goes on, back to where she started. The playground becomes twisted in itself and enables the reader to walk on both sides of the field without crossing any lines.

The peculiar thing is that although the reader thinks she is walking straight ahead, she is unconsciously walking along both sides of the strip and traveling twice the assumed distance, which is the circumference of the non-twisted strip. In terms of the reading process, the book plays with the reader by sending her along a plot-line, which is twisted and self-discursive, and demands twice the reading effort compared to other books just to let her 'finish' at the same point where she started. The fact that the reader only realizes this after an odd thousand pages of laborious reading is almost ironic. She might have sensed that there cannot possibly be any comprehensive conclusion to the book, but being referenced back to the start is not just ironic but also somewhat depressing.

The play of infinity and jest creates an area of tension, which the reader risks getting lost in it. Just as Hal is not able to find a way out of the centre, the reader is not able to find an exit out of the book. Her attempt to entirely consume or even digest this piece of entertainment would necessarily have to end in a state of *cosmopsis* just like every "drive to an all-encompassing comprehension of reality in fact closes the individual off from the world around." (van Ewijk 2009: p.138) Every effort to fully understand the novel, to categorize it, or to deal with the cosmic view, would be connected to so many unmanageable implications that the reader would get totally lost like Hal, unable to get up and read on. In Hal's case, he is not even able to make himself understood anymore. When he is sitting in an application interview for another tennis academy in the 'first' episode of the book, all that comes out of his mouth are crazy, animal-like sounds. Even after having read the whole book, the reader does not know why this is the case. One possibility is that Hal might have ingested a heavy drug called 'DMZ' or 'Mme Psychosis'. The other option is that Hal is not able to find an exit from his prison, which is his own mind; a mind twisted like a Möbius strip. In order to fully digest the book, the reader would have to read on and on, without finding any conclusive point, till one day she would pass away. This admittedly exaggerated interpretation of play between infinity and jest shows that the book *Infinite Jest* seems to share some essential features with the mysterious movie *Infinite Jest*. The reader would end up exactly like the paralyzed victims of the lethally addictive entertainment that was made by Hal's father James Orin Incandenza.

J.O.I. is one of the most mysterious characters that appear in *Infinite Jest*. He leads an exciting and eventful life in which he is a successful tennis player, a masterly scientist in the field of optical physics, the founder of the Enfield Tennis Academy, and probably the most unconventional filmmaker of his time. Although James O. Incandenza was an expert and perfectionist in each of his fields of occupation, the most interesting aspect for this study is his *œuvre* as a filmmaker and his unique conception of what entertainment is and how it should be made. Looking at his initials, J.O.I., one might assume that Incandenza's name stands for pure, unconditional entertainment. But considering the tragic last years of

J.O.I.'s life, namely his serious drinking habit and his spectacular micro-wave-suicide, one can already guess that he was not a very entertaining type of man per se. On the other hand, "anyone with a nervous system who watched much of his oeuvre could see that fun or entertainment was pretty low on the late filmmaker's list of priorities." (p. 791) Nevertheless, he was the inventor of the 'anti-confluential' movie, which made him the leading figure of the "'après-garde' experimental and conceptual film work [being] too far either ahead of or behind its time, possibly, to be much appreciated at the time of his death in the Year of the Trial-Size Dove Bar." (p. 64) J.O.I.'s anti-confluentialism violates every common principle of film-making that has evolved around Hollywood's *classical continuity*. These principles "assure that the spectator understands how the story moves forward in space and time." (Bordwell 2006: p.119) In contrast to that, the spectator of a typical Incandenza has nothing that assures her of what is happening on the screen. This lack of a common film-language is why J.O.I.'s movies were on the one hand heavily criticized and on the other hand celebrated by different critics, both for the same reason. A hostile critic would probably argue that J.O.I.'s works cannot possibly be taken seriously neither in terms of their entertainment value nor for their artistic demand. The most controversial example for this and at the same time the most hated title from J.O.I.'s filmography is the movie *The Joke*. The ads and posters for this film displayed a disclaimer that strongly advised the audience *"NOT To Shell Out Money to See This Film."* (p. 397) Those people who were still keen to see the movie involuntarily became part of an audience-specific event, which is described in J.O.I.'s filmography as follows:

> "[T]wo Ikegami EC35 video cameras in theatre record the 'film' 's au-
> dience and project the resultant onto screen – the theatre audience
> watching itself watch itself get the obvious 'joke' and become increas-
> ingly self-conscious and uncomfortable and hostile supposedly com-
> prises the film's involuted anti-narrative flow." (p.988)

Soon after the 'release' of *The Joke,* J.O.I. went even further when he invented the "hostilely anti-Real genre of 'Found Drama,' which was probably the historical zenith of self-consciously dumb stasis." (p.398) The eleven episodes of Found Drama that J.O.I. produced are anti-real to the extent that they are only "conceptual, conceptually unfilmable [and] UNRELEASED." (p.990) At the same time they are in fact real since J.O.I. used the real everyday life of random people as his plot. Therefore he pointed out a name from a telephone book at haphazard and declared everything that happened to this person during the next 30 minutes as being the Found Drama. The hostility of this genre is based in its total exclusion of all audiences, the neglecting of a scripted plot, and the anti-creational role of the artist himself.

Strictly speaking, Found Drama is an ultimately real art form because it has no camera that distorts reality according to Heisenberg's uncertainty principle. It is the uncertainty that hinders the viewer from differing fiction from reality. When Mario for example walks through E.T.A. with a camera on his head in order to shoot a documentary he is not sure if the people he is filming are acting or really talking to him. "Mario directs the lens at Chu's shower-thongs so he can look over the viewfinder at Chu. 'Are you saying this, or is this what happened?'" (p. 759) Nevertheless, there remains a problem with Found Drama, which is the sobering fact that something which claims to be real actually becomes untellable and thus remains nothing more than an idea, or rather a concept. This makes unconditionally true and real art almost impossible. For most of the characters in the book, this dilemma even extends to their whole concept of reality, which is why "real stuff can only get mentioned if everybody rolls their eyes or laughs in a way that isn't happy." (p. 592) This abstraction of reality is what drives many of the characters to take drugs, creating a sort of parallel reality for themselves, which saves them from an enduring state of *anhedonia* or simple melancholy.

> "Kate Gompert always thought of this anhedonic state as a kind of radical abstracting of everything, a hollowing out of stuff that used to have affective content. Terms the undepressed toss around and take for granted as full and fleshy – *happiness, joie de vivre, preference, love* – are stripped to their skeletons and reduced to abstracts. They have, as it were, denotation but not connotation." (p.693)

Hal's *cosmopsis* can also be defined as a form of *anhedonia,* in which his infinite abstraction of the world around him makes it impossible for him to continue his tennis career at E.T.A. Just like an anhedonic patient, Hal is able to denote things like grief or happiness and to act according to common expectations in order to deliver the goods. Nonetheless, he is not able to evoke the correct connotations meaning that his constant fake attempts to satisfy everyone's claims make him actually "far more robotic than John Wayne." (p. 694) But even though Hal was a rather successful 'faker', highly intelligent and talented on the court, he felt the same "gnawing sense of worthlessness" (p.693) as the rest of his fellow students. Unfortunately, "[t]he idea that achievement doesn't automatically confer interior worth is, to them, still, at this age, an abstraction, rather like the prospect of their own death – 'Caius is mortal' and so on." (p.693)

This questions the whole idea of the novel. If real art can never leave the conceptual phase, than every piece of written work, like *Infinite Jest* for example, automatically becomes unauthentic. The text would always be in opposition to its mere existence. When the reader realizes this fact she might as well feel the 'gnawing sense of worthlessness' of her reading effort as she advances through the book without ever really reaching the bottom of things. The principle of uncertainty applies here as well since the reader never knows quite where she stands. Just like J.O.I.'s audiences she might get the feeling that something seems to be wrong with the text; some hidden joke that becomes more and more apparent to her and that might even turn into hostility towards the text. The book, as well as the movies, have one thing in common.

They are both

> "[t]echnically georgeous [...] with lightning and angles planned out to the frame. But oddly hollow, empty, no sense of dramatic *towardness* – no narrative movement toward a real story; no emotional movement toward an audience. Like conversing with a prisoner through the plastic screen using phones." (p.740)

Of course I would not go so far as to declare a thousand pages of literature to be totally empty, but still there is this lack of *towardness* that hinders the reader from fully identifying with the characters and really getting involved in the story. The uncertainty remains and is amplified by the already discussed structural complexity that might be exhausting for the reader but is still "an absolutely necessary element of the [reading] experience." (Aubry 2008: p.215)

Even more important than the similarities between J.O.I.'s movies and the book are their differences. Interestingly enough, *Infinite Jest* is a tremendously entertaining book to read even despite its complexity, whereas James Incandenza himself referred to his movies as 'entertain-ments' only "ironically about half the time." (p. 743) The irony here is the play of the gross stasis of some of J.O.I.'s films and their entertainment value, which is based on another performance of play, namely that of the professional technical realization of the films and the anti-narrative quality of their content. This specific performance of play can also be adapted to the reading process of the book. The play establishes itself between two poles that Wolfgang Iser calls the *artistic* and the *aesthetic*.

> "The literary work has two poles, which we might call the artistic and the aesthetic; the artistic refers to the text created by the author and the aesthetic to the aesthetic realization accomplished by the reader. [...] The work is more than the text, for the text only takes on life when it is realized, and furthermore, the realization is by no means independent of the individual disposition of the reader." (Iser 1988: p.212)

The reader slips into the role of a player who performs between the structurally complex artistic pole and the idiosyncratic aesthetic pole. This is another way to describe the playground of reading in which the rules of the game are established through the reader's discourse with the text. So in contrast to Timothy Aubry who wrote that *Infinite Jest* offers "decon-structive games" (Aubry 2008: p.215) it might be more appropriate to talk about reconstructive games in which a Barthian reader takes the role of the author and makes it possible for the text to 'occur'.

Just as J.O.I. was "obsessed with the idea of audiences' relationships with various sorts of shows," (p.396) the relationship between the reader and the novel becomes an integral part of the book itself. The reader herself, with her individual disposition and her idiosyncratic ways of approaching the book, becomes part of the whole show. In contrast to a chronologically ordered, linear narration, which is held together by a structured plot-line, *Infinite Jest* only becomes complete through the individual reading experience, which is a performance of play. The same thing can be said about prototypical anti-confluential works of J.O.I. A movie like *The Joke* for example just would not work without the audience watching themselves, becoming more and more self-conscious and thus uncomfortable.

This changed in the last phase of J.O.I.'s creative activity when he was desperately trying "to make something that ordinary U.S. audiences might find entertaining and diverting and conducive to self-forgetting." (p. 944) It was the time when he filmed *Infinite Jest*, the lethally addictive entertainment. This movie reversed the concept of a maximally self-conscious audience into an audience that should forget about themselves, avoiding every form of self-confrontation. Curiously, J.O.I. originally conceptualized the movie especially for Hal. Since he realized that his talented son was somehow trapped inside his own world which he could not enter, he tried to find a way to 'save' him.

> "To concoct something the gifted boy couldn't simply master and move on from to a new plateau. Something the boy would love enough to open his mouth and come *out* – even if it was only to ask for more. [...] Make something so bloody compelling it would reverse thrust on a young self's fall into solipsism, anhedonia, death in life." (p.839)

He wanted to use Hal's innate inner child, which could not bear down its drive for entertainment, to get Hal out of himself and to be able to really get in touch with his son. Unfortunately, his experiment was a failure since everyone who ever only got a glimpse of the movie became trapped in the same fierce prison of the mind as Hal, with death being the only exit. It is not the audience that completes the work here; it is the movie that completes the audience. The entertainment is actually so stimulating that the consumer remains infinitely happy until she dies. Here, the word 'jest' takes the meaning of 'taking charge of' or of 'carrying something', presumably the reader. The movie gains control over the subject who in return loses power over herself. It is a game of choice that no one can ever win. In this game the consumer can decide whether to watch to the movie or not, and if she decides to she never has to make any decision again.

According to Marathe, a member of a Canadian separatist group, there is not even the choice to watch the movie or not.

> "[N]ow is what has happened when a people chose nothing over themselves to love, each one. A U.S.A. that would die – and let its children die, each one – for the so-called perfect Entertainment, this film. Who would die for this chance to be fed this death of pleasure with spoons, in their warm homes, alone, unmoving." (p.318)

In Marathe's view, the American's "drive for spectation" is bigger than the fear of dying, meaning that the satisfying their personal appetite for entertainment becomes their most important aim in life. That is why different groups in *Infinite Jest* try to get hold of the master copy of the Entertainment, which seriously endangers the citizens of the Organization of Northern American Nations, whose acronym 'O.N.A.N.' underlines this common urge to fulfill one's desires that Marathe was speaking of.

What remains unclear, for *a priori* reasons, is the exact content of the movie. There is simply no one who could tell the reader what really happens in *Infinite Jest*. Nevertheless, the book contains some snippets and individual scenes that are narrated by Mme Psychosis, who does not just have the name of a heavy drug but is also a recovering drug addict and the main actress in the movie.

> "In the first scene I'm going through a revolving door. You know, around this glass revolving door, and going around out as I go in is somebody I know but apparently haven't seen for a long time. [...] And instead of going in I keep going around in the door to follow the person out, which person is also still revolving in the door to follow me in, and we whirl in the door like that for several whirls." (p. 939)

Although the actress is steadily whirling through the revolving door, she is neither entering nor exiting. She is doing both things at the same time. Almost ironically, despite all her effort she is not able to reach her goal, which is to talk to the familiar person. Just like on a Möbius Strip, where the reader 'reads along' the surface in order to find something, the revolving door becomes both: origin and end. It becomes a symbol of J.O.I.'s death cosmology, which is explained in the next scene. Mme Psychosis is sitting nude in front of the camera

> "explaining in very simple childlike language to whomever the film's camera represents that Death is always female, and that female is always maternal. I.e. that the woman who kills you is always your next life's mother." (p.788)

So Mme Psychosis is a female incarnation of death that leads the viewer through the revolving door of life's departure, which then turns out to also be an entrance to a new life with the figure of death as the new mother. Because dying is still a rather traumatic experience the rest of the movie consists basically of Mme Psychosis apologizing to the viewer. "[T]here were at least twenty minutes of permutations of 'I'm sorry.'" (p.939)

The last interesting fact about the movie *Infinite Jest* is that it was filmed with a specially designed 'wobble-lens'. The point of view of the whole last scene, which makes the viewer believe that she is lying in a cradle, combined with the wobbly vision of this special lens, are intended to "reproduce an infantile visual field." (p.940) Thus the central point of *Infinite Jest* is to make the audience believe that they are in fact helpless infants that are taken care of by Mme Psychosis. This reciprocal relationship between the movie and the audience, as well as between life and death, are further performances of play of infinity and jest. The aspect of infinity lies in the eternal cycle of being born and dying; a revolving door that is neither only inside nor outside, and that we cannot get out of. Jest in this context takes another etymological meaning, namely 'to bear or to carry', whereas 'carry' refers especially to a child in the womb. The play of infinity and jest reduces the viewer to a powerless object, which cannot take care of itself and is constantly being carried by the maternal figure of death. And that is what actually happens when someone watches the movie. The poor victim loses the ability to take care of herself, surrenders all responsibility for her own person until she is finally led out the revolving door of life into a new one. This satisfies a secret need of adults living in the O.N.A.N. In one episode of the book Hal accidentally visits a self-help Group for adult men, who are trying to live out their inner infant's desires. After being asked by the Group leader to name what their inner infant wants right now more than anything in the world, one of the Group members answers "*To be loved and held!*" (p.803) In contrast to the reading process of the book *Infinite Jest*, in which the reader and the book carry each other, the movie *Infinite Jest* does not need the viewer's support. This means that the Entertainment is not really a Derridean centre. The play of infinity and jest does in fact not end but is still being performed while the viewer watches the movie. Unfortunately, the viewer is not able to engage in this process anymore. She is not just held by the Entertainment, she is held captive by her own personal centre with no chance of ever escaping again. The consumer becomes consumed by the medium.

Interestingly enough, the Entertainment was only meant as a joke. The whole project was drafted and realized by J.O.I. under the premise of being ironic. The problem was that "it was too perfect to release – it'd paralyze people." (p.940) The joke became in fact so consummate that no one was able to pick up on the irony. That is why the movie became the lethally addictive entertainment, which leads to the question as to whether the book *Infinite Jest* is perhaps nothing more but the longest joke in the world that does not even have a punch line. J.O.I. was in fact called a "shitty editor of his own stuff" (p. 947) for the boredom and the impatience that his static movies triggered in the audience. Concerning the book one could also argue that it was badly edited due to its numerous lengthy passages. The reader might in a way even feel betrayed when she finishes the book. Betrayed for all the time she has invested in the tedious reading of such a complex work only to realize that nothing is resolved at the end and that it even starts again from the beginning. She feels like a drug addict whose habit "had long since stopped being a release or relief or fun." (p. 22) The complexity of the text, which is designed as a "virtual addiction apparatus [...] is to bring the readers into a state of dazzled intellectual fatigue, a state which might take them ready to embrace salutary simplicity offered by addiction's potential antidote, Alcoholics Anonymous (AA)." (Aubry 2008: p. 210)

AA in *Infinite Jest*, which is the last plot-line of the book that I will discuss in this paper, is not just the antidote to drug addiction, it is also the anti-pole to everything else in the book. It is an irony free zone, which offers a totally "alternative set of values, centered around simplicity, empathy, and sincerity." (Aubry 2008: p. 206) The sincere and simple values represented by AA's rules and regulations finally make it possible for the reader to lose her feeling of uncertainty about the novel and give her something that is ultimately real and authentic. The Ennet Halfway House is "very real; people are crying and making noise and getting less unhappy, and [Mario] once heard somebody say God with a straight face." (p. 591) But on the other hand it is this very authenticity that makes the place "not just un- but *anti*-interesting" (p. 358) for everyone living there. Nevertheless, it enables the reader to fathom out the novel and to touch the ground of it. Instead of being confronted with tons of information that has to be processed, all that remains is "about a dozen basic suggestions" (p. 356) that every Group member has to follow. Thus, the Ennet Halfway House becomes the total opposite of the entertainment society of the O.N.A.N. Instead of constantly looking for the perfect entertainment and hunting the next kick, the members of AA just wait for the next Group meeting, hoping stay clean with the help of the Group's familial support. The structure offered by this family has some parallels to life at E.T.A. But a crucial distinction between the two institutions, besides the difference between the detoxification of drug addicts and tennis coaching of young kids, is that the students at E.T.A. can decide whether they want to be a part of the game or not. The residents at Ennet House do not have any alternative but to join AA.

In AA lingo, the point at which an addict actually enters the house is referred to as "hitting bottom." (Aubry 2008: p.213)

> "You are, as they say, Finished. You cannot get drunk and you cannot get sober; you cannot get high and you cannot get straight. You are behind bars; you are in a cage and can see only bars in every direction. You are in the kind of a hell of a mess that either ends lives or turns them around. You are at a fork in the road that Boston AA calls your Bottom." (p. 347)

This bottom is the common ground where the reader and the addicted characters from the book meet each other, and where neither of which becomes paralyzed by the malady *cosmopsis*. That is due to the fact that there are simply no more than two options left at this point, which is either to "do it or die." (p. 357) This is an *anti-cosmoptic* situation that contrasts with the otherwise complex moments of decision-making in *Infinite Jest*. All the addict can do is surrender to the rules of AA in order to be saved from a death warrant. This is a different situaion to life at E.T.A., where the students surrender to the rules because they *want* to be a part of the game and later a part of The Show. The Ennet House residents cannot decide if they want to play or not, they just have to. If we consider AA as being a game where the addict's life is at stake, then winning for the addict means sheer surviving. The addict has to surrender to a Higher Power and give up her self-determinedness, which is mirrored in the 12th step of the official AA commitments 'Giving it Away'.

"Giving it Away is a cardinal Boston AA principle. The term's derived from an epigrammatic description of recovery in Boston AA: 'You give it up to get it back to give it away.'" (p. 344) The addict has to give up her substance and put herself into the hands of the Group. "The word *Group* in *AA Group* is always capitalized because Boston AA places enormous emphasis on joining a Group and identifying yourself as a member of this larger thing, the Group." (p. 1025) In the same way that Hal gets lost in a game that is bigger than himself, the drug addict soon realizes escaping her addiction is a task too big to be carried out by herself. The Group will then help her to get *it* back; *it* being the ability to live a relatively normal life again. This is under the condition that the Group member gives it back again, shares it with the other members of the Group and makes it possible for newcomers to also get it back. Unfortunately, this is a circle that never really ends. It is a play of infinity and jest in which the Group carries the addict out of her chemical addiction into a social form of dependency that she is not able to get out either. It is an infinite performance of play, since there are Group meetings every day and the members are not allowed to miss them out. Even after years of sobriety the addict has to attend these meetings and slip into the role of the so-called 'Crocodiles' in order to guide newcomers through their first drug-free year. Thus, AA cannot be seen as way out of addiction, it is rather a substitute; a door that says exit and in fact turns out to be an entrance.

The addict is not the only one who walks through this door. As the reader 'takes part' in more and more Group meetings while she is reading the book, she also becomes a member of this Group. Although AA is not a place where people actually want to end up in real life, it gives shelter to the reader and represents her only place of refuge in the book. The Group meetings can only work if everyone sticks strictly to the truth. Everything that is said "has to be the truth unslanted, unfortified. And maximally unironic. An ironist in Boston AA is a witch in church." (p. 369) It is the unconditional frankness of AA Group members which makes it possible for the reader to fully identify with all the Ennet House residents and to share their individual destinies. This makes AA the negation of the ultimately ironic movie *Infinite Jest*. In this movie the viewer should be hindered from identifying with the appearing character. Mme Psychosis was even wearing a veil that hid her face since "it wasn't important" and not meant "to be captured realistically by the lens." (p. 940) Ennet House staff member Gately chooses the complete opposite approach.

> "Gately's found it's got to be the truth, is the thing. He's trying hard to really hear the speakers — he's stayed in the habit he'd developed as an Ennet resident of sitting right up where he could see dentition and pores, with zero obstructions or heads between him and the podium, so the speaker fills his whole vision, which makes it easier to really hear." (p. 369)

Gately needs to see the person standing up front in order to fully identify. The narrator in return needs the audience's reaction in order to actually occur up there. It is a process that connects the audience with the narrator. In contrast to this, the viewer of *Infinite Jest* enjoys the movie on her very own without realizing anything that is going on around her. She becomes trapped in herself. AA represents the complete opposite since it releases people from their personal prisons and gives them a second chance inside the sheltering collective of the Group.

What holds this Group together and what enables its members to identify with each other is the last performance of play that I will discuss. It is a play of infinite jest, which is based on the ongoing narrative performance of each member of the Group. 'Jest' cannot just mean 'story (orig. in verse)'; it can also mean 'to perform' or 'to accomplish'. That is exactly what happens each night at any arbitrary Group meeting. Somebody stands in front of the Group and performs as a narrator of his or her personal story of addiction. The others listen to the story, trying to identify with each other. They support the narrator by cheering 'Hang In!' or 'Keep Coming!' and thus suggest that this narrative play will go on forever. This resembles the oriental fairy tales of *One Thousand and One Nights*. The story which forms the framework of this collection of tales is about the beautiful Scheherazade and sultan Sheriban. Once upon a time the sultan ordered that each night he wanted to sleep with another fresh virgin, who should be put to death every next morning after the defloration. Scheherazade wanted to stop the sultan from killing in this senseless manner and decided to spend a night with him as well. After they slept with each other Scheherazade starts to cry because she wants to say goodbye to her sister Dinarsarde. When her sister arrives she asks Scheherazade to tell one of her delightful stories. So Scheherazade starts to tell one of her stories but does not reveal the end of it. The sultan, who wants to know how the tale ends, does not kill Scheherazade but asks her to come back the next night to finish her story. But Scheherazade does not just finish her first fairy tale; she even tells another unfinished story that saves her life for a second time. And so it goes on for 1001 nights until the sultan finally falls in love with Scheherazade and asks her to be his wife.

The narrative play of AA works just like Scheherazade's trick. The addicts gather almost every night and "are asked to tell their story in front of a group of fellow members as well as listen to the experiences of the others." (van Ewijk 2009: p.134) If they stopped coming to these meetings to share their stories they would relapse into their addiction and probably die. Death was also the constant threat that made Scheherazade come back each night to tell her stories. At AA another important factor is that the audience tries to identify with the narrator without simply comparing themselves. This would not work in any case since every story told at AA is unique and comparing would only lead back to a weak self. So everybody tries to identify and to build up a strong community that carries each of its members. The *homo chemicus* turns into a *homo narans*.

In this context one could argue that the Ennet House is not the irony-free zone that it first seemed to be. The irony might be excluded from the AA agenda but it is still implicit in the mere existence of the institution and in its bromidic rules. This irony is performed by a play of antagonisms. The first one is that the addiction, the original cause of becoming an AA Group member, is never really cured. It is just replaced by a pre-structured life, which is ordered by a set of seemingly brainless platitudes. That means that even AA, the only real antidote of *Infinite Jest*, offers no exit that could release the reader from being implicated in the reading game. Although the reader happily embraces the radical simplicity of AA she will not find a conclusion to the infinite play of jest. Just like any Ennet House resident she has to surrender to a Higher Power in order not to lose track even if she does believe in this Power or not. Gately for example, who did not believe in a Higher Power either, said about his faithless and automated daily prayer that "talking to the ceiling was somehow preferable to imagining talking to Nothing." (p. 467) Gately has to live according to rules and values that he does not even believe in, which is ironically the only way for him to keep sober day after day after day. In order to be free from addiction, he has to surrender to the rules of the game at AA. This means that Gately has to give up his self-determinedness and become a group-determined person in order to win back his life. A Group that is taken charge of and carried by this very game of infinite narration.

David Foster Wallace's *Infinite Jest* is the textual realization of this game of infinite narration. Whereas the interaction between infinity and jest in the book can often be depicted as a lose performance of play, the reading process itself is a game in which the reader competes with the book. In this context, the length of the novel is just the conversion of this infinite game into prose. The game starts as soon as the reader begins her journey through the book, which also completes the text as an entity. The paradox of being implicated in this game is the same as being a member of a Boston AA Group. In order to Make *it* one has to agree to the terms and conditions set out by the game. Making *it* in this context can have several meanings. It could simply mean that the reader actually finishes the book, which is hard to accomplish not just because it is so long but also because it has no real ending. But Making *it* could also mean that despite the length and the complexity of the book the reader can still find answers to some very important questions, namely 'what to love?' and 'what to give yourself up for?'. At the end of the day, *Infinite Jest* remains a book about the pursuit of happiness and thus about the things that bother us daily and deeply touch us.

And in search of some answers to these questions, the reader acts just like a Boston AA Group Member; she Hangs In and Keeps Coming back to the text day after day in order to play the game of infinite jest. The fact that this game cannot be won by the reader is not because the book is an opponent that cannot be defeated, it is because the game simply never ends, even after she has finished reading. The true aspect of infinity becomes apparent in everything that goes beyond the text and the reading process. The end of the text becomes the origin of a new game that involves and changes the reader. Of course there is no text that leaves its reader unaffected, but *Infinite Jest* actually changes the way a reader approaches a book and perhaps even life itself. After reading *Infinite Jest* one truly realizes that neither life nor a text can ever be finite. Just like the book our life is open-ended. *Infinite Jest* extends the reader's idea of what a novel can do by giving her the insight that reading is by no means a unidirectional process. It is a game. And in this game the reader and the text constantly challenge each other. Sometimes the reader might not feel challenged by the text at all; then again the complete opposite might be the case. However, in the context of a game, being faced with a strong opponent might make the other player feel inadequate and depressed. But even if she gets defeated this is the only way to improve and grow as a player. Curiously enough, in terms of the book, the prerequisite to this growth is the loss of the reader's self-determinedness and her immersion into the reconstructive performances of play that carry her through the book. Although *Infinite Jest* challenges the reader to an extreme extent and even if it might seem that she has to surrender to the complexity of the game, at the end she will be set free and reborn as a grown, self-determined individual. Grown not just in her role as a reader, but as a human being.

Bibliography

Aubry, Timothy. 2008. "Selfless Cravings – Addiction and Recovery in David Foster Wallace's *Infinite Jest*". In: Prosser, Jay (Ed. 2008) *American Fiction of the 1990s – Reflections of History and culture*. London: Routledge.

Barth, John. 1988. *The End of the Road*. New York: Anchor Books.

Barthes, Roland. 1977. *Image Music Text*. New York: Hill and Wang

Berger, Arthur Asa. 1997. *Narratives in Popular Culture, Media, and Everyday Life*. Thousand Oaks, CA: Sage Publications.

Birkerts, Sven. 1996. "The Alchemist's Retort – A multi-layered postmodern saga of damnation and salvation". *The Atlantic Monthly,* February 1996.

Bordwell, David. 2006. *The Way Hollywood Tells It – Story and Style in Modern Movies*. Berkley, CA: University of California Press.

Böttger, Miriam. 2009. "Unendlicher Spaß von David Foster Wallace"
ZDF Aspekte, August 22nd, 2009.
<http://www.zdf.de/ZDFmediathek/beitrag/video/823754>.
Accessed: March 22nd, 2010.

Bresnan, Mark. 2008. "The Work of Play in David Foster Wallace's *Infinite Jest*". *Critique*, Vol. 50, No. 1, Fall 2008.

Derrida, Jacques. 1966. "Structure, Sign and Play in the Discourse of Human   Sciences". In: Rice, Philip & Waugh, Patricia (Ed. 1992) *Modern Literary Theory. A Reader. 2nd Edition.*
London: Edward Arnold.

Freund, Wieland. 2009. "Als David Foster Wallace die Spaßgesellschaft portätierte". *Welt online*, August 17th, 2009.
<http://www.welt.de/kultur/article4336191>.
Accessed: March 22nd, 2010.

Hayles, N. Katherine. "The Illusion of Autonomy and the Fact of Recursivity: Virtual Ecologies, Entertainment, and 'Infinite Jest'". *New Literary History*, Vol. 30, No. 3, Summer 1999.

Iser, Wolfgang. 1988. "The Reading Process: A Phenomological Approach". In: D. Lodge (Ed.), *Modern Criticism and Theory: A Reader*. White Plains, NY: Longman.

McCaffery, Larry. 1993. "An interview with David Foster Wallace". *Review of Contemporary Fiction*, Vol. 13.2, Summer 1993.

Noland, Richard W. 1966. "John Barth and the Novel of Comic Nihilism". *Wisconsin Studies in Contemporary Literature*, Vol. 7, No. 3, Autumn 1966. Madison, WI: University of Wisconsin Press.

Patridge, Eric. 1961. *Origins - A Short Etymological Dictionary of Modern English*. London: Routledge.& Kegan Paul.

Van Ewijk, Petrus. 2009. "I and the Other: the Relevance of Wittgenstein, Buber and Levinas for an Understanding of AAs Recovery program in David Foster Wallace's Infinite Jest". *English Text Construction*, Vol. 2, No. 1. Amsterdam: Benjamins.

Wallace, David Foster. 1996. *Infinite Jest*. New York: Back Bay Books.